MY BRAIN IS POWERFUL

WRITTEN BY
LAUREN E. MUNROE
MSED, NCSP, CAS, BCES, CCTP

ILLUSTRATED BY
IAN GONZALES

My Brain is Powerful
Lauren E. Munroe MSEd, NCSP, CAS, BCCS, CCTP
Published 2022
Munroeschoolpsychologist@gmail.com
ISBNs 979-8-88759-048-6 - paperback
979-8-88759-049-3 - ebook

This book belongs to:

_____

To Wyatt, may you always know how powerful you are.

My name is Sam and I want to tell you about my brain and my body.

We all have a brain.
Your brain is inside of your head and is protected by your skull.
Did you know that your brain keeps your whole body going
and controls everything that you do? Even how you think and learn!

BRAIN SCANNER 5000

Learning seems easy for everyone except for me. Why does my brain work like this? Is it broken? Do I need someone to fix my brain?

Sometimes I feel like I can hear all the sounds around me. Like the phone ringing or even someone tapping their pencil. It makes it so hard for me to pay attention.

Mom and dad know that I try my best.
My teacher knows that I try
my best too, but sometimes my body moves too fast,
and making the right choice is hard.

Mom said she knew just the right person who could help, Dr. Dana.

Dr. Dana told me that my brain is not broken, it is powerful and one-of-a-kind!

BRAIN SCANNER 5000

Dr. Dana told me that in our brain, we have something called neurotransmitters. Neurotransmitters are messengers that send signals throughout our body. These signals affect how we breathe, feel and learn.

Neurotransmitter, the body's messenger

Dr. Dana told me that everyone's brain works differently. We all need something different to keep our brain balanced and strong.

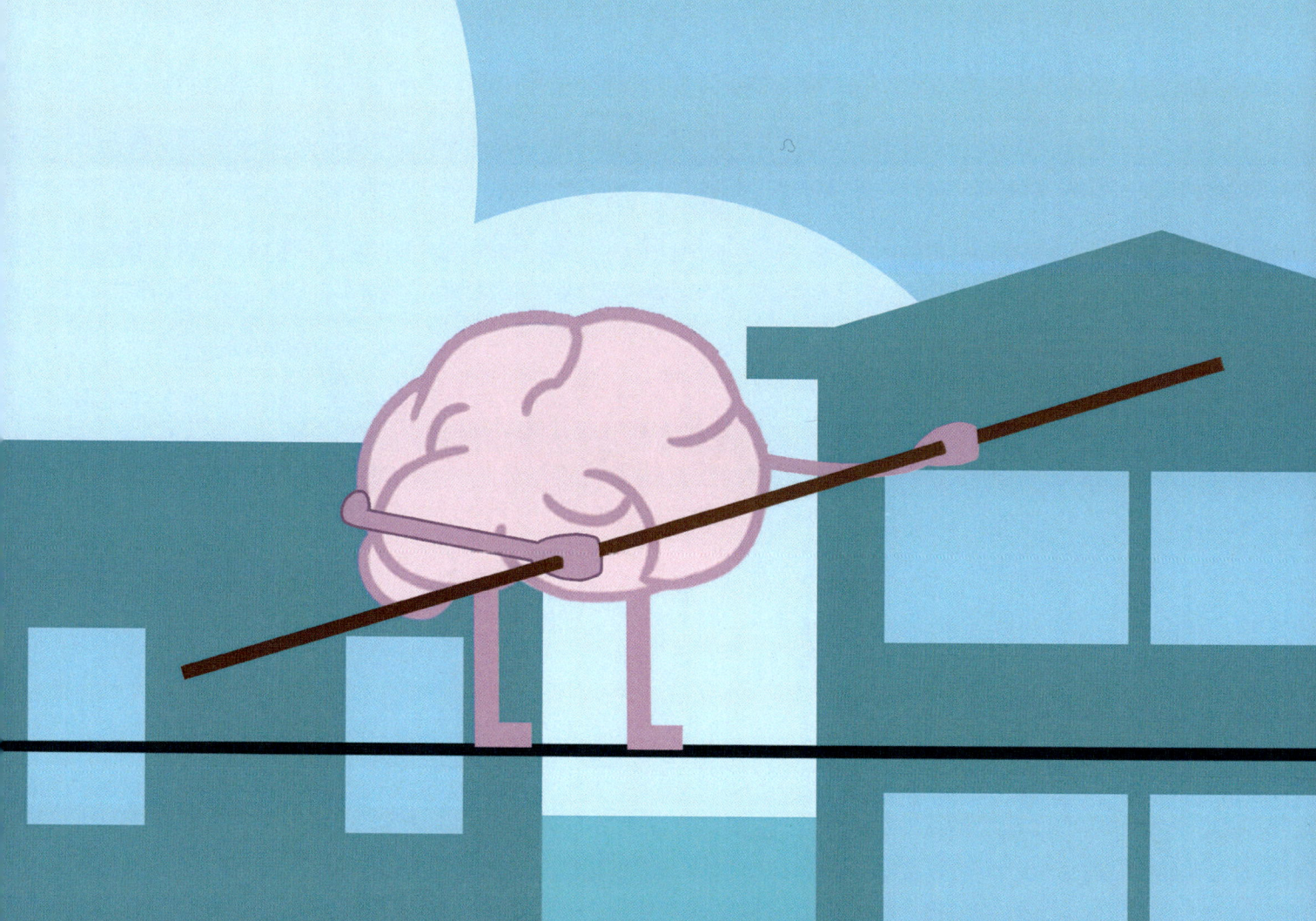

She told me that it is important to practice using strategies to calm my body when I feel that I am starting to lose control.
We practiced taking deep breaths, counting to 10, and imagining my favorite place.

I can take a body break and think about how my body feels.

Jogging

Jumping Jacks

I can use my words or use a picture to share how I feel.

I feel sad

Dr. Dana prescribed a medication for me that helps how messages are sent throughout my body. She said this could help me slow down and feel less wiggly.

I have so many strategies now.
I keep them in the toolbox in my brain.

Your toolbox helps keep your brain balanced and strong.
My brain is powerful and yours is too!

ACTIVITY PAGE

1. How do you you feel? Write it or draw it on the line.
2. Cut 3 visuals from below and tape/glue onto the boxes.

I feel _____

My Strategies
I can...

1.

2.

3.

- Count to 10
- Drink water 
- Take deep breaths 
- Take a body break 
- Think of a happy place

ACTIVITY PAGE

I feel _____

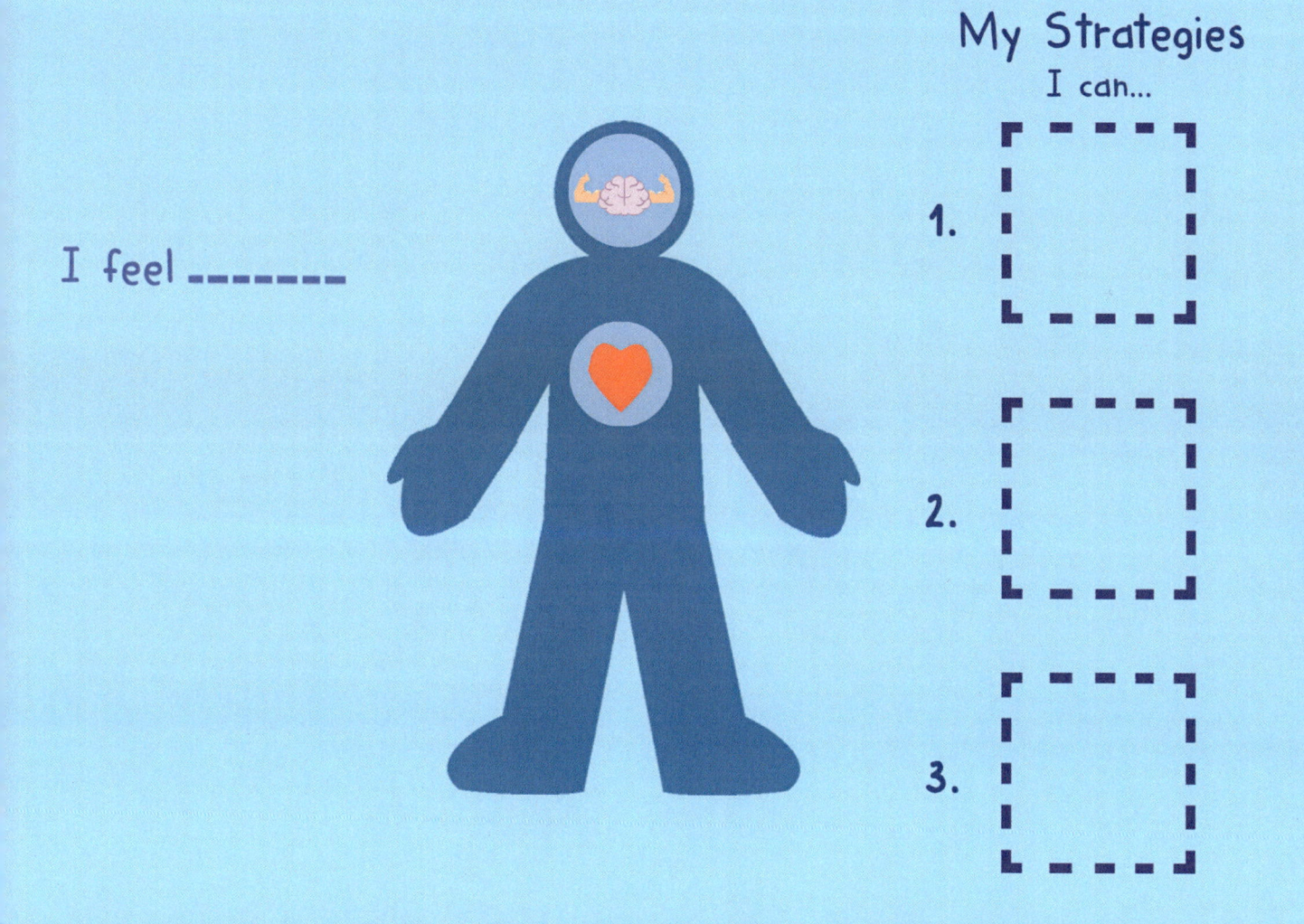

My Strategies
I can...

1.

2.

3.

Count to 10  | Drink water  | Take deep breaths  | Take a body break  | Think of a happy place

What tools can you use?

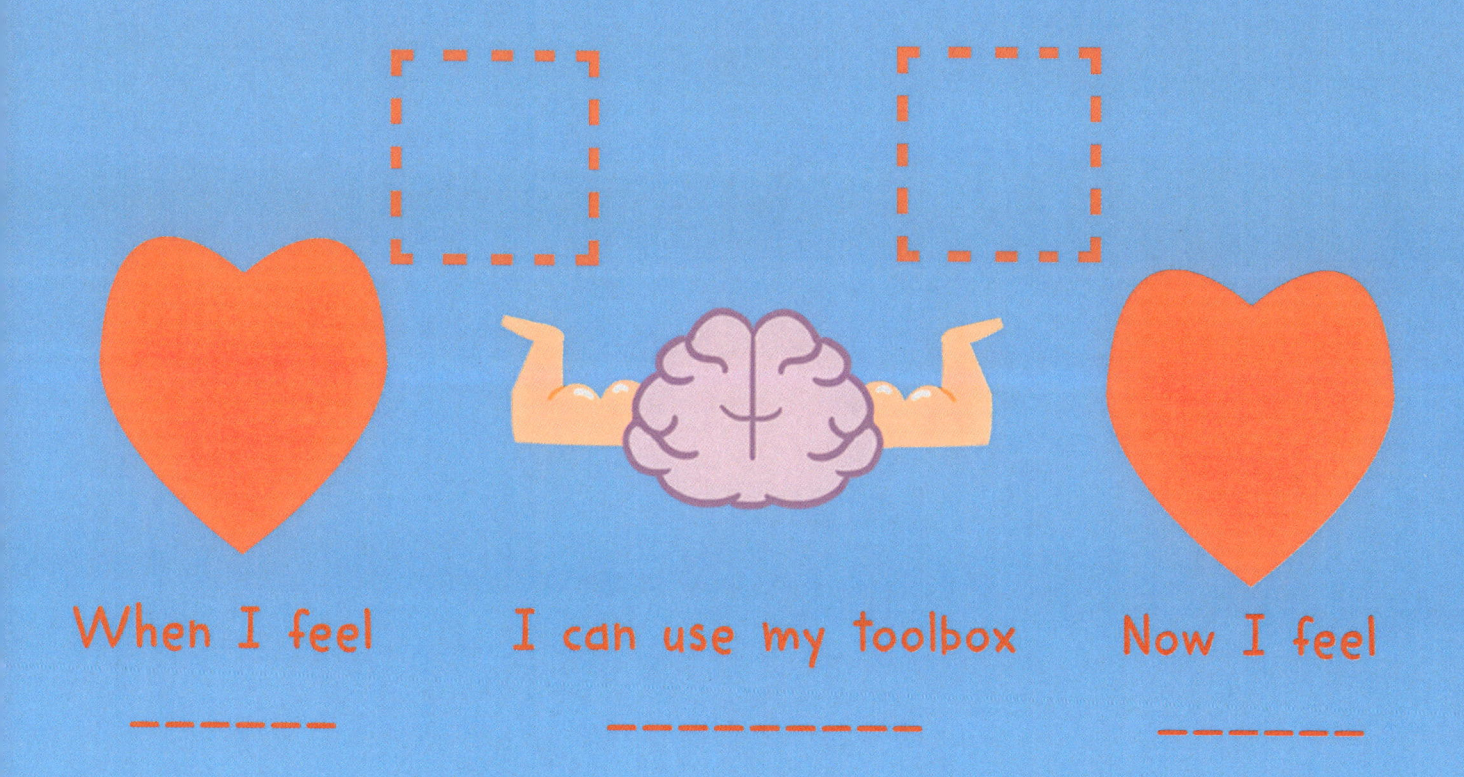

When I feel _____   I can use my toolbox _____   Now I feel _____

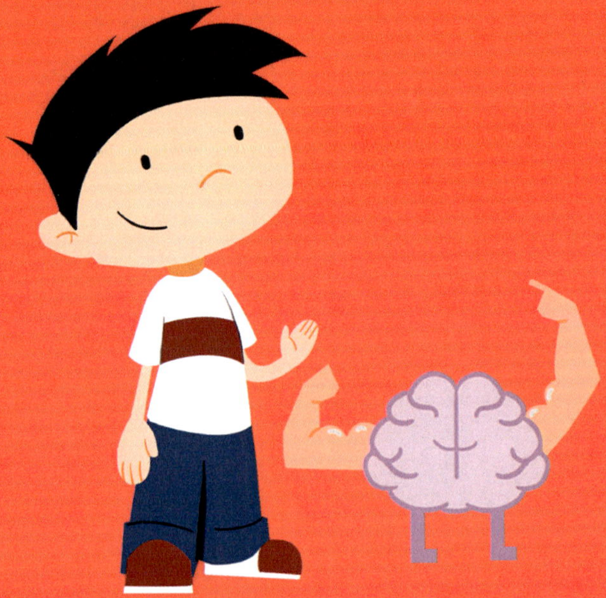

ABOUT THE AUTHOR
LAUREN E. MUNROE

Lauren is a wife, mom, dog mom, and school psychologist who loves spending time with her family, going on bike rides, running, and the beach. She has extensive experience working with neurodivergent learners, specifically students with autism, ADHD, and other developmental delays. She is passionate about providing children with inclusive opportunities so they feel supported and empowered to learn. She hopes this book will be a resource that normalizes each person's unique journey and the toolbox they used along the way.

Made in the USA
Las Vegas, NV
13 April 2025